WERE YOU THERE?

FIND YOURSELF WITH JESUS

WERE YOU THERE?

FIND YOURSELF WITH JESUS

PAINTINGS

RON DICIANNI

STORIES

NEIL WILSON

Were You There?

Text copyright © 2004 by The Livingstone Corporation.

Paintings copyright © 2004 by Ron DiCianni.

Published by Integrity Publishers, a division of Integrity Media, Inc., 5250 Virginia Way, Suite 110, Brentwood, TN 37027.

HELPING PEOPLE WORLDWIDE EXPERIENCE *the* MANIFEST PRESENCE *of* GOD.

Scripture quotations are taken from the *Holy Bible*, New Living Translation, copyright © 1996. Used by permission of Tyndale House Publishers, Inc., Wheaton, Illinois 60189. All rights reserved.

Produced with the assistance of The Livingstone Corporation (www.LivingstoneCorp.com). Project staff includes Kirk Luttrell, Madison Trammel, Dave Veerman, Neil Wilson, Mary Horner Collins, Mark Wainwright.

Interior design by The Livingstone Corporation.

Cover design by Brand Navigation | www.BrandNavigation.com

ISBN 1-59145-211-2

Printed in USA
04 05 06 07 08   RRD   7 6 5 4 3 2 1

TABLE OF CONTENTS

INTRODUCTION

Thousands of us have enjoyed Ron DiCianni's artistic reflections on Scripture. His paintings have a quality that creates indelible memories. His work helps us answer the question, "Were you there?"

One fall day several years ago I spent an unforgettable couple of hours wandering through the Billy Graham Center in Wheaton, Illinois, mesmerized by the way Ron's artwork forced me to think about the Bible in new ways. He made the familiar accessible. He captured biblical events in a manner that not only made me recognize them, but also invited me to participate in them. He brought biblical themes to contemporary settings and helped me apply those truths. His meditations in paint allowed me to find myself in Scripture and reminded me of the ways Scripture can live in me.

As the designated writer for this project, I am personally indebted to Ron for his skillful renditions of God's Word. His paintings have given me a new appreciation for the Scripture's depths. It struck me anew that the more we keep coming back to the Bible and the closer we study its contents, the more likely we are to find ourselves in its pages. God's Word will, in Paul's words, show us "what is true and make us realize what is wrong in our lives. It [will] straighten us out and teach us to do what is right."

The paintings you are about to experience function in several ways. Some present profound biblical moments such as Jesus' temptation in the wilderness or the return of the prodigal. Others offer convicting encounters with an enduring truth, such as Jesus and a modern figure observing the widow who gave a small but noteworthy gift. Still others present contemporary applications of biblical principles, such as a mother and son sharing a moment of solitude while an angelic guardian looks on, unnoticed.

Each of the stories inspired by these paintings offers a specific "reading" of the image intended to assist your biblical meditation. Sometimes you will hear a figure in the painting speak. Other times you will meet an unseen observer. These glimpses of Scripture made me appreciate the way God preserved his Word. For example, the painting of Jesus in the wilderness reminded me that no one had witnessed Jesus' conflict with Satan; one of the disciples must have asked Jesus later to describe what had happened. Similarly, the snapshot of the prodigal's return, with the father and son embracing and a smaller figure rushing toward them in the background, could portray the younger son's return or, perhaps, the later repentance of the older son. As you step deeper into the biblical narratives, you will find your imagination fired with possibilities and applications you've never seen before.

Ron and I believe wholeheartedly that our work is no substitute for Scripture. We pray that what we have done will simply invite you to closer observation of God's Word.

So enjoy this book with your Bible open. Savor the context and background of these paintings and stories. Read the Bible passages with your imagination turned on. Visualize the biblical truth in a contemporary setting. See the compelling, unchanging, and persistent human issues in particular historical events. As you do, we are convinced that you will discover, again and again, that you were there.

We trust that our efforts will encourage you to meet Christ anew every day. Once you find yourself with Jesus in the Scriptures, he will guide you to tell your story, paint your pictures, proclaim your message, and live the life he has planned for you.

NEIL WILSON
Resurrection Season, 2004

Gabriel's
Message

But the angel said, "Don't be afraid, Zechariah!
For God has heard your prayer, and your wife, Elizabeth,
will bear you a son! And you are to name him John."

— LUKE 1:13

God is more anxious to bestow his blessings on us

than we are to receive them.

— ST. AUGUSTINE, EARLY CHURCH
BISHOP AND THEOLOGIAN

GABRIEL'S MESSAGE

LUKE 1:13

He swallowed slowly, reliving the terrifying and wonderful moment. I knew my own dry throat matched his. Zechariah looked at me, expecting me to doubt what had happened, like others he had entrusted with his treasured encounter. His eyes were wide open and brimmed with tears, desperately wanting me to read in his face what his mouth could not put into words. He grunted in surprise when he saw my expression. I couldn't help but smile back at him as I reached out and held his leathered,

bearded cheeks in my hands. After a moment, a look of recognition came over his face. Yes, I knew exactly what he was grunting, gesturing, and blinking about. I knew about inexpressible treasures. I had my own startling encounter with Gabriel to marvel over.

Elizabeth, old enough to be my grandmother yet giddy enough to be my sister, sat nearby and laughed at both of us. Her hands rested on her belly as she said, "Zechariah, you old oak, it looks like you have almost as much

in common with Mary as I have with her." At five months, she could no longer hide the pregnancy she was so pleased about. Changes in my own body told me a miracle had begun to grow in me, too. The last few queasy mornings confirmed that the baby was real and my life would never be the same again. I shivered with anticipation, delight, and a vague sense of dread at becoming a mother.

I looked down again at the parchment Zechariah had handed me. On it, in shaky lines, he had recorded his encounter with Gabriel, the same angel who had visited me. Already in awe over his chance to represent the people in the Holy of Holies, Zechariah had considered himself a blessed man to step through the curtain into God's very presence. He was so concerned with avoiding disrespect in his duties that it never occurred to him God might honor him with a personal messenger. Gabriel's appearance was shocking enough, but the message he delivered left Zechariah

I knew about inexpressible treasures. I had my
own startling encounter with Gabriel to marvel over.

trembling. Not only would he and Elizabeth bear a son in impossibly old age, but that son would set in motion the central act in God's plan to make things right with the world.

For me, the choice had been clear. Gabriel's message was too wonderful not to be true. I knew I was only expected to accept it. I wondered what had been so hard for Uncle Zechariah that Gabriel had taken his voice. I asked. His weathered features squinted in response. He sighed, shrugged, and shook his head. He slipped the parchment from my hands and scribbled his answer.

"I guess this old oak needed to be quiet for a while. My time for shouting will come when John is born."

I read his explanation aloud, so Elizabeth could laugh some more. And I could almost hear Gabriel in the distance, laughing with her. ✝

Not only would he and Elizabeth bear a son in impossibly old age, but that son
would set in motion the central act in God's plan to make things right with the world.

For those who are willing to receive them, God's best gifts often arrive unexpectedly.

Are you willing to be surprised by God with a new, unanticipated—and perhaps even scary!—blessing?

THE NATIVITY

But when the right time came, God sent his Son, born of a woman,
subject to the law. God sent him to buy freedom for us who were slaves
to the law, so that he could adopt us as his very own children. ... [Mary]
wrapped him snugly in strips of cloth and laid him in a manger,
because there was no room for them in the village inn.

— G A L A T I A N S 4 : 4 - 5 ; L U K E 2 : 7

This is the irrational season
When love blooms bright and wild
Had Mary been filled with reason
There'd have been no room for the child.

—MADELEINE L'ENGLE, AUTHOR

THE NATIVITY

GALATIANS 4:4-5; LUKE 2:7

I remember vividly the first time I met Paul and his traveling companions. I had heard stories about their previous visit from those who had become Christ-followers, and my friend Timothy said he was planning to offer his services to Paul when he passed by again. My first glimpse of Paul revealed a scruffy, scarred, and sickly traveler gesturing and thundering in the marketplace of Lystra. But his message captured me. Paul's words about a savior sounded so good—it seemed I had been looking for Jesus all my life.

As I stood in the market that day, I noticed one of Paul's friends next to me. He introduced himself as Luke. Compared to Paul's theatrics, Luke's demeanor was quiet and calm. I thought that he and Paul formed an unusual partnership. Luke held a tablet and took notes while Paul spoke. Since I couldn't write, Luke offered to teach me a little if I would help him remember everything that went on that day.

Later that evening, I discovered that Luke had assembled a collection of scrolls recording

his notes. He told me that God had led him to interview many of the people who had known Jesus before and after his resurrection. Luke said he was compiling a careful account of Jesus' life. I was fascinated. Luke opened a tattered skin and murmured, "This is my favorite. I spent several days with Jesus' mother." Then he gently waved the roll in the candlelight. "These are her accounts of the Savior."

As if knowing my wishes, Luke unrolled the scroll and began to read about the birth of Jesus. I have heard the story repeated many times since then, but that first time changed everything for me. The simple account of a miracle among ordinary people spoke volumes about God's timing. I still carry a mental picture created by the story of the King's birth. The circumstances might have seemed all wrong to some people, but they were divinely right to God. God's timing created a masterpiece from a miracle.

I have heard the story repeated many times since then, but that first time changed everything for me.

The simple account of a miracle among ordinary people spoke volumes about God's timing.

Three figures fill my mental canvas: Mary, Joseph, and the child. In my imagination, bright moonlight casts shadows around the simple animal shed, giving everything a blue tint. Along with his mother and father, I, too, am drawn to the newborn. We sit still and silent, hoping this moment will not pass, yet knowing that without the moments to come, this moment would mean nothing. For the child can't stay a child. He has come for a reason.

Even now I am moved to tears when I think about that particular baby, born at that particular moment, who changed me. The marvelous and unique miracle of his birth made countless spiritual births possible, including mine. The king arrived under the cover of moonlight and humanity to save his creation. His timing was perfect. His plan was a masterpiece. ✝

I am moved to tears when I think about that particular baby,

born at that particular moment, who changed me.

Jesus' birth demonstrates God's wild,
irrational, sacrificial love for you.

Have you made room
for him in your life?

HEAVEN'S LOSS

They ran to the village and found Mary and Joseph.
And there was the baby, lying in the manger. ... Mary quietly treasured
these things in her heart and thought about them often.

—LUKE 2:16, 19

Come, my Way, my Truth, my Life!

Such a Way as gives us breath,

Such a Truth as ends all strife,

Such a Life as killeth Death.

— GEORGE HERBERT,
17TH CENTURY POET

HEAVEN'S LOSS

LUKE 2:16, 19

The deep darkness of the early morning lingered, and I had yet to sleep. The excitement couldn't alleviate my weariness from many miles of travel and tension, followed by the anticipated but unexpected birth of the child. Mary and I were thrilled and exhausted. She even more than I. Even the angelic visits months ago hadn't quite prepared us for the events of the evening. Our late arrival had left us homeless. Then the birth-pains began, and I pled for shelter from an innkeeper who kindly offered his stable. I was a beggar who couldn't be a chooser, but Mary seemed confident that the One who had led us this far must have a purpose.

The birth, painful but swift (though I'm not a good judge of such things), brought us an honor beyond expression. I held Mary's Son as if he were my own, knowing with trembling awe whose Son he really was. And then, no sooner had we cleaned up the child and wrapped him against the night chill, when out of the darkness came shepherds excited to share the most

fantastic story of angels giving them directions to the child. They tenderly passed our baby around, giving glory to God. Then they left, eager to tell others what had happened.

After Mary had fed Jesus for the first time, I noticed how mother and baby nodded contentedly and slipped into sleep. I tried to lift the child gently but still startled Mary awake. "Hush," I whispered. "I'll lay him in the manger again while you sleep." She nodded, too tired to show resistance. By the time I had Jesus nestled in the feed box, she was asleep again in the hay.

I lay down myself, below the level of the manger, and lost sight of the baby. All was quiet, and I knew that sleep would soon overtake me as well. Gazing past the temporary wooded crib, I marveled at the starry night. I

I held Mary's Son as if he were my own, knowing

with trembling awe whose Son he really was.

couldn't help but chuckle when I noticed a tiny arm, flung out in sleep, appear over the edge of the manger. I wondered if that was the motion he had used when scattering the stars in the heavens.

Barely awake, I thought of previous generations of my forefathers who had slept under these same skies, hoping and waiting for the child that I could now reach out and touch. I thought of all the promises and disappointments through the years. God had needed to shape my people with sadness and suffering. But lying in the hay above me was God's final answer. When I had sobbed his name the first time, I had simply followed the angel's instructions: "We shall call him Jesus, for he will save his people from their sins." I surrendered to sleep, certain that angels would keep watch. ✝

I wondered if that was the motion he had used

when scattering the stars in the heavens.

Where do you go with your hurts, your questions, your disappointments?

Celebrate the coming of the Way, the Truth, and the Life. Welcome him anew. Worship.

THE SHEPHERDS'
VISIT

*"And this is how you will recognize him: You will find
a baby lying in a manger, wrapped snugly in strips of cloth!"*

— L U K E   2 : 1 2

The Word was made "flesh" so that the wisdom of God could
come within the reach of human beings. . . . The Word, the Son of God,
put on a humble, human form, so that infinite truth could be seen in finite terms.
— ST. AUGUSTINE,
EARLY CHURCH THEOLOGIAN

THE SHEPHERDS' VISIT

LUKE 2:12

Edging a little closer to the fire, I wrapped my cloak tightly around me and cleared a few small rocks out of the way in order to give me just enough space to lie down. My brother was already soundly asleep. I'd finished my turn; now Dad would handle the late-night watch over the sheep. I could just make out his silhouette as he sat looking up at the crisp night sky. The crackling of the fire and the occasional bleating broke the stillness. Light glinted from the stars above and a few scattered oil lamps in the village of Bethlehem below. I settled into my space, closed my eyes, and nodded off.

Suddenly I was on my feet, heart pounding, startled and confused. A dazzling light illuminated every rock, sheep, and blade of grass. I stood terrified and looked around and above. I saw my dad—he seemed scared, too. But then, out of the light, a voice told us, "Don't be afraid!"

Not that I've ever seen one before, but I

immediately knew that this was an angel. He told us that he had great news—the Savior, the Messiah, the Lord had been born that night in Bethlehem! He said we would find him as a baby, lying in a manger. Suddenly the light shone even brighter as a sky full of angels joined in, singing glory to God. Then, just as quickly as they had appeared, they were gone. Our eyes took a few moments to adjust to the sudden blackness. We looked at each other and had the same thought. Quickly we made our way down, winding around the sheep, and then sprinted toward Bethlehem.

From what the angel had told us, we thought we should look for a stable. We ran past dark stables, disturbing their occupants and evoking whinnies and moos. The town was packed with traveling visitors. Dodging around carts, we ran up and down every street.

Then we saw it. Behind an inn that appeared to be bursting at the seams, a light streamed from the stable. This must be the

He told us that he had great news—the Savior, the Messiah, the Lord had been born

that night in Bethlehem! He said we would find him as a baby, lying in a manger.

place. Almost reverently, we stopped. Nearly exhausted from the search, we could see our breath in the cool air. Then we walked toward the light. A man inside the stable heard us. He didn't seem surprised to see us; in fact, he beckoned us forward.

Just as the angel had said, the baby was there, in the manger. I dropped to my knees and looked into that tiny face. *This is the Messiah?* I thought. *But he's so small and helpless!*

And *it's a boy, just like me.* I wondered what he would be like when he grew up. How would he save our people?

I don't know how long we lingered. Eventually, we turned to go—back to our sheep and our normal lives. But nothing would ever be "normal" again. I had a story to tell, and I began to tell it to everyone who would listen as we walked back to the hillside. I had seen the Savior! ✠

I dropped to my knees and looked into that tiny face.

This is the Messiah? *I thought.*

You, too, have received a personal
invitation to see the Savior.

Will you come?
Will you spread the Good News?

SIMEON'S MOMENT

Simeon was there. He took the child in his arms and praised God, saying,
"Lord, now I can die in peace!
As you promised me,
I have seen the Savior
you have given to all people."

—LUKE 2:28–31

O honoured and venerable Simeon, thou earliest host of our
holy religion, and teacher of the resurrection of the faithful,
be our patron and advocate with that Saviour God, whom
thou wast deemed worthy to receive into thine arms. We, together
with thee, sing our praises to Christ, who has the power of life and death.

—METHODIUS OF OLYMPUS,
EARLY CHURCH SCHOLAR

SIMEON'S MOMENT

LUKE 2:28–31

Simeon was there, in the Temple, almost every time I attended. I came driven by guilt; he always seemed filled with joy and anticipation, as if expecting to meet God personally among the bustling crowds in the courts. If possible, my own expectations were directly opposite Simeon's. I desperately hoped I wouldn't encounter God, because that would make me face who I had become. I wasn't ready for that.

I wondered over Simeon's secret. What could make someone so exuberant about God?

Simeon managed to be holy without mustiness or pretension. Sure, he was old and frail, but his ancient bones seemed to vibrate with life. His weathered features, stooped shoulders, and shuffling gait somehow struck me as temporary restrictions on a soul of boundless energy and joy. His faithfulness to God and his eagerness over God's plans for our miserable people drew me to Simeon. I wanted to be like him. He had a reason to be here; I still hadn't found mine.

Then one day in the Temple, just when I

thought things couldn't possibly get better for Simeon, they did. I was close by when he spotted a couple with a baby and a dove cage making their way to the sacrifice area. I didn't notice anything special about the young family, but Simeon seemed to recognize them. The couple appeared surprised when he approached them excitedly. His face glowed as he stood before the woman and reached out. As the young mother slowly extended the newborn bundle, a shadow of anxiety crossed her lovely features. It vanished as Simeon took the child in his arms and began to praise God.

Simeon's gravelly voice rumbled and soared in a shout that echoed above the common roar of the Temple courts. "Lord, now I can die in peace! As you promised me, I have seen the Savior you have given to all people. He is a light to reveal God to the nations, and he is the glory of your people Israel!" Somehow, coming from Simeon, these momentous words were an announcement to be taken at face value. The old man had waited

The old man had waited a lifetime for
this moment, and it had arrived.

a lifetime for this moment, and it had arrived.

Having made his triumphant declaration, Simeon seemed spent. He silently gazed into the face of the child in his arms before tenderly placing the precious bundle back in the mother's care. I was near enough to hear the sadness in his voice as he added, for the couple's benefit, some wistful words of blessing. I didn't catch all of what he said, but one phrase struck like an arrow in my soul: "This child will be rejected by many in Israel, and it will be their undoing. But he will be the greatest joy to many others." The words pierced me with an unavoidable choice. I had to choose to respond to God's light and plan as revealed in this child, or I had to finally reject God. I suddenly realized the hope that had given Simeon life. In that moment I closed my eyes and joined Simeon. I chose life. I chose to pin my hope on this baby who I came to realize was God himself in human flesh. Simeon's moment allowed me to find a reason for being here.

The words pierced me with an unavoidable choice. I had to choose to respond to God's light and plan as revealed in this child, or I had to finally reject God.

Have you, like Simeon,
longed for deliverance,
for forgiveness,
for the Savior?

He came for Simeon.
He came for you.
Receive him with joy!

THE FORERUNNER

In the book of the prophet Isaiah, God said,
"Look, I am sending my messenger before you,
and he will prepare your way.
He is a voice shouting in the wilderness:
'Prepare a pathway for the Lord's coming!
Make a straight road for him!'"

— M A R K   1 : 2 - 3

Repentance is the golden key that opens the palace of eternity.
—JOHN MILTON, BRITISH POET

THE FORERUNNER

MARK 1:2-3

Zechariah didn't say much. At first, he had a good reason—he was mute. For nine months he could only gesture, nod, and write in dust or on parchment. Later, after the boy was born, he tried to explain what had happened to him, but we only half-listened. I mean, Elizabeth's late autumn pregnancy had most of us in the village kidding Zechariah mercilessly. It was hard for us to accept what the old priest claimed about his son. God certainly had shown his strange sense of humor to an elderly couple. Yet our history reminded us that the near-miracle wasn't out of character for God. And although none of us had been visited by an angel, we had precedents in our ancestry. We often wondered what little John might have to do with the rest of us.

The boy grew like a weed. An intense child, he spent hours alone, wandering the hills. He always seemed to be looking for something or someone. Zechariah and Elizabeth died during his childhood, but the boy didn't seem bothered by the solitude that became his life.

Before we knew it, word began to trickle back to the village that John was stirring things up in the wastelands. How could someone so young get into so much trouble so quickly! We wondered if perhaps the desert had stolen his soul. From all appearances he might have been a madman, living in the wilderness on insects, clad in the rough skins of camels. He was a sight to see, and more. The restlessness we had sensed in him as a child had erupted into pas-sionate preaching from a grown man. People even said he sounded like Elijah. Now *that* sent ripples across the land!

John wasn't hard to find. You just followed the crowds to the place where the wilderness met the Jordan. You felt yourself strangely drawn by his disquieting message. "Repent!" he shouted. Then he named sins and sinners. I know many went to hear John excoriate religious leaders, but the Baptizer seemed, in time, to include every-

It was hard for us to accept what the old priest claimed about his son. . . .
Yet our history reminded us that the near-miracle wasn't out of character for God.

one in his convicting messages. Those who approached as spectators often ended up in the water with John, asking for baptism.

When the voice crying in the wilderness started raising eyebrows in Jerusalem, John's message became a nuisance to some. Herod had him arrested. The next thing we knew, John had lost his head. But though his voice was silenced, his message continued to ring.

John had stirred up a mood of anticipation from the heights of Golan to the Dead Sea.

And John had a cousin. Now people are saying that Jesus is following in John's footsteps. Others say that John called Jesus the "Lamb of God who takes away the sin of the world!" Well, John always said someone would follow him who we really ought to follow. I wonder if he meant the Nazarene. ✠

You felt yourself strangely drawn by his disquieting message.

"Repent!" he shouted. Then he named sins and sinners.

Are you, like John, a mouthpiece for God?
Do you speak his words
to the people around you?

Why was it necessary for John
to preach repentance before Jesus
could preach salvation?

Is there anything you need
to confess to God?

Temptation of Jesus

*Then Jesus, full of the Holy Spirit, left the Jordan River. He was led by
the Spirit to go out into the wilderness, where the Devil tempted him for
forty days. He ate nothing all that time and was very hungry.*

— L U K E   4 : 1 - 2

He who with his whole heart draws near unto God

must of necessity be proved by temptation and trial.

— ALBERT THE GREAT,
DOMINICAN SCHOLAR

TEMPTATION OF JESUS

LUKE 4:1-2

I don't remember who actually asked Jesus about it. All of us wondered at one time or another about the forty days he had spent in the wilderness following his baptism. Someone finally posed our question. "Lord, what happened while you were away after John baptized you?" He looked away, eyes reflecting the flames of our warming fire. Stillness settled on us. Before he began, his eyes swept the room, searching our faces. When he looked at me, I felt as if he was asking, "How much will you understand, how much should I tell you?" He told the story simply, as if to make sure that we remembered the details.

It was bad enough to go into the wilderness to see and hear John. But, at least, other people were always around. Besides, John was wild enough to somehow fit in that place. When Jesus told us the Spirit had led him into the wastelands alone, most of us shivered. We certainly didn't pass through wilderness spots unaccompanied. We instinctively avoided those

places. And we figured our ancestors had spent enough years there to make up for any of the rest of us.

The Jesus we knew wasn't afraid to be alone. He snatched moments of privacy as often as we would let him, but we understood these were times alone with his Father, not at all like his first time in the wilderness.

And, as it turns out, Jesus wasn't alone there. He was harassed and tempted by Satan. In three different ways the tempter tried to get Jesus to betray his identity, to go along with

When he looked at me, I felt as if he was asking,

"How much will you understand, how much should I tell you?"

Satan's will rather than his Father's. Jesus described his victory using phrases that were as familiar to us as our mother's lullabies. He had quoted God's word to defeat temptation. If the words of Scripture were Jesus' weapons, they could certainly be ours.

As difficult as the loneliness, the temptations, and the forty-day fast may have been, Jesus spoke of that time with deep feeling. It sounded like contentment to me—like the satisfaction of an exhausting fight won. ✝

If the words of Scripture were Jesus' weapons,

they could certainly be ours.

Have you ever felt hounded or forsaken?
Lost in the wilderness? Remember, Jesus said
he will never leave you or forget you.

Jesus suffered and faced temptation
just as you do. He understands
your weakness, and he loves you anyway.
Bring your cares to him.

THE LEPER

Jesus reached out and touched the man.
"I want to," he said. "Be healed!"
And instantly the leprosy disappeared.

— LUKE 5:13

The good Instructor, the Wisdom, the Word of the Father,

who made man, cares for the whole nature of his creature.

The all-sufficient Physician of humanity, the Savior,

heals both our body and soul....

— CLEMENT OF ALEXANDRIA,
EARLY CHURCH SCHOLAR

THE LEPER

LUKE 5:13

I had been unclean for as long as I could remember. I couldn't tell you the last time someone had touched me, and I wouldn't have been able to feel it if they had. I was a leper. People kept their distance.

The terror of leprosy was the absence of pain. I couldn't tell by touch if an object was sharp, rough, hot, or cold. Pain never told me to stop doing something that was causing damage to my body. I walked on a wounded foot until it became a stump. I burned myself badly and scratched myself raw without even noticing. The ugliness of a leper was a symptom of the disease. We couldn't feel.

But we did feel. We felt the deep shame of rejection. The loss of family, friends, and human fellowship mangled our souls. The company we kept with other lepers highlighted our misery. Every day we had to announce to anyone who came near that we were unclean. We could not escape the humiliation.

Naturally, I first heard of Jesus from a distance. Rumors of his power reached even those of us on the edges of society. His words were said to change hearts, and he healed sicknesses of every kind. I looked at the ugly thing that my body had become and wondered: *Could he make me feel?* I wouldn't mind the scars I carried if he could restore my bodily pain and relieve the pain within.

When I heard that Jesus was on his way to the village, I made sure I was as close to the road as the rules permitted. I expected to call out for his attention when he passed me. Instead, he noticed me right away. Yet, he didn't turn his head in disgust or walk to the far side of the road. Instead, he turned and walked toward me. As desperate as I was to talk to him, the old habits and fear had me shouting "unclean" as he approached. He didn't seem to hear. I was suddenly overwhelmed with my own unworthiness to have one so holy draw so near.

I fell with my face in the dust, partly to

His words were said to change hearts,
and he healed sicknesses of every kind.

hide my shame and partly to protect him. In that moment I knew I could not demand or deserve the healing I desired. It was entirely his choice. I tried to let him know I understood that when I murmured, "Lord, if you want to, you can make me well again."

I saw the tips of his sandals approach as he stood over me, silent. A hand appeared in the corner of my eye and it closed on mine, lifting me from the ground. My instinct was to resist, but the wonder at being touched overwhelmed me. He said, "I want to. Be healed."

Like a wave of fire, the nerves throughout my body flared. Starting with the hand he touched, wholeness swept through me. The pain was delicious—it hurt. Scars vanished, sores closed, badly damaged limbs tingled with renewed strength. With crystal clarity I knew that as long as I trusted Jesus, I would never be unclean again. ✝

In that moment I knew I could not demand or deserve

the healing I desired. It was entirely his choice.

*Are you in need of spiritual,
emotional, or physical health?*

*Come to Jesus and experience
his healing touch.*

THE TRUTH

*"Don't misunderstand why I have come. I did not come to abolish
the law of Moses or the writings of the prophets.
No, I came to fulfill them."*

— MATTHEW 5:17

Long my imprisoned spirit lay
Fast bound in sin and nature's night
Thine eye diffused with quickening ray
I woke, the dungeon flamed with light.
My chains fell off, my heart was free
I rose, went forth, and followed Thee.

— CHARLES WESLEY,
METHODIST HYMN WRITER AND PREACHER

THE TRUTH

MATTHEW 5:17

*M*oses towered over me. Though long dead, the shadow cast by his life still seemed to hover over every part of mine. All my brightest and darkest days were measured by the laws laid down by my great ancestor. In my mind, Moses' face always carried a stern look of disapproval. He carried the famous stone tablets in his hands, and I imagined they were completely covered with hundreds of finely chiseled commandments. Moses' laws covered everything. Comments that began with "Moses said" had an uncanny way of producing almost instant guilt. Then I met Jesus.

What amazed me about Jesus was the way he could begin talking about very familiar subjects but end up showing me I had completely missed the point of what I thought I understood. For example, I heard him deliver what we all called the "Sermon on the Mount." During that sermon, he mentioned the Law of Moses several times. I knew the Law of Moses. Or, I thought I did.

Jesus shifted gears in the middle of his message. "Don't misunderstand why I have come. I did not come to abolish the Law of Moses or the writings of the prophets. No, I came to fulfill them." Moses never stood taller than that moment. His shadow pressed down on me. Yet, listening to Jesus, I realized that much I had believed was Moses' law actually boiled down to someone else's idea of how the Law should be applied to life. The way our teachers explained the Law wasn't wrong; it was just too narrow. Sometimes the rules were so letter-perfect that they missed the main point, the spirit of the Law. At other times the instructions created contradictions between different parts of the Law. These were resolved in ways that dishonored God's character. The pile of laws we tried to juggle made God look arbitrary, selfish, and angry, rather than gracious, firm, and loving.

All my brightest and darkest days were measured by

the laws laid down by my great ancestor.

Jesus helped me see that we had underestimated the Law. God's Law wasn't out of touch; it was out of reach. God's Law wasn't something we could break; it was a rock that broke us. Taken seriously, the Law drove me to Christ. Any attempt to measure my life according to the Law was sure to result in failure. I needed supernatural help.

As I sat listening to Jesus describe the terrible beauty of the Law, I suddenly realized that he towered over Moses. Jesus lived the Law, because the Law described his character. If Jesus could live through me, I would be free—not free from the Law, but free to live by the Law for Christ's sake.

That was the moment I put my faith in Christ. I still live in Moses' shadow; but both of us live in the shadow of Jesus, and we get along just fine. ✝

Jesus helped me see that we had underestimated the Law.

God's Law wasn't out of touch; it was out of reach.

Jesus came so that you might have freedom—not freedom from God's standards, but freedom to live and thrive within their bounds.

Are you experiencing Christ's freedom today?

THE SINNER

*"I tell you, her sins—and they are many—have been forgiven,
so she has shown me much love. But a person who is
forgiven little shows only little love." Then Jesus
said to the woman, "Your sins are forgiven."*

—LUKE 7:47-48

In these days of guilt complexes,
perhaps the most glorious word in the English language is
"forgiveness."

— BILLY GRAHAM, EVANGELIST

THE SINNER

LUKE 7:47-48

At first, I stood outside, feeling unwelcome. I knew Jesus was approachable. But I also knew that those who were with him were not. Some of them knew me in ways I was ashamed to remember. Their hard looks seemed to blame me for things we had done together in the dark. Others knew my reputation. But Jesus knew me in a different way, a pure way, and my previous meeting with him had left me feeling understood, accepted, and forgiven. I longed for a way to express my gratitude.

The party seemed like a poor opportunity to honor Jesus. Too many judgmental minds might question my motives or decide to humiliate me. But as I watched them through the window, interacting with Jesus, I realized they were treating him as disrespectfully as they had ever treated me. I saw the false courtesy of their invitation revealed in their rude remarks and lack of genuine welcome. Something in me wanted to be near this one who was willing to endure such abuse from those unworthy of his company.

I slipped into the room and knelt in the one place I thought should have been crowded. But the floor at Jesus' feet was empty. Overcome with emotion, my tears flowed, and it seemed somehow right to let them fall on Jesus' feet, streaking the dust. But I needed more liquid to wash the residue of travel from his toes and heels. I reached in my robe and my fingers closed on a precious vial of perfume sealed in an intricate, hand-blown bottle.

As I pulled out the vial and prepared to break the stem, I heard a gasp. That's when I realized that the room had fallen silent. I, who had hoped not to be noticed at all, was now the center of attention. Though the shame of my past instantly returned to accuse me, I refused to be ashamed of the one who had set me free from the past. I cracked the slender glass and slowly poured out the fragrance, filling the room with an indescribable scent.

But Jesus knew me in a different way, a pure way, and my previous meeting with him had left me feeling understood, accepted, and forgiven.

Then I wiped Jesus' feet with my hair. Lost in the wonder of the moment, I didn't realize he was speaking until he gently placed his hand on my head in a gesture of blessing. As I looked into Jesus' eyes, I saw that he understood what I was doing better than I. He saw me better than I would ever see myself. For a split second, in the glow of his gaze, I caught a glimpse of his view of me. Clean, pure, spotless within and without, pouring out a fragrance of praise from the broken remnants of my past.

I continued to kneel at Jesus' feet with my head bowed, sensing that he could see my soul in uncluttered adoration. He declared me accepted, my love received, my past forgiven. Hidden in the enclosure of my hair, streaked with the precious dust I had wiped from his feet, I couldn't help but smile at the unexpected glory of the moment. He turned my tears into laughter. ✠

As I looked into Jesus' eyes, I saw that he understood what I was

doing better than I. He saw me better than I would ever see myself.

Do you need Jesus' forgiveness?
He never rejects a sinner who comes
to him in repentance and humility.

Reflect on the mercy that God
has shown you. How can you extend
God's mercy to others?

THE SOWER

*"I, the Son of Man, am the farmer who
plants the good seed. The field is the world, and the
good seed represents the people of the Kingdom."*

— MATTHEW 13:37-38

Preach the gospel everyday; if necessary, use words.

— FRANCIS OF ASSISI,
FOUNDER OF THE FRANCISCANS

THE SOWER

MATTHEW 13:37-38

I've reached a place in life where I can look back without panicking. I have regrets, but I'm willing to mention them if they might help someone else avoid a mistake I've made. Mostly, I look over my shoulder in gratitude.

People often declare that hindsight is 20/20, but I think hindsight may be more perceptive than simple vision. Looking back allows us to see patterns that are rarely apparent in day-to-day life. Backward glances can't change the past, but they can influence the present and future. The mirror of memory helps prevent repeated mistakes.

Viewed over my shoulder, I notice in a very different way the impact others have had on my life. I can see that opportunities and choices were presented to me by people who appeared in my life as if planted there. Often, brief conversations, counsel, and direction came from these fellow travelers. They, in turn, introduced me to others who also influenced my journey. A number of them helped me to get to know Jesus.

I can see clearly now that Jesus arranged a number of encounters in my life. Instead of speaking directly to me, he often sought my attention through other people. They, in turn, sowed into my life the words of Jesus. They were part of a tilling process that made me feel like farm soil. I mean, some of these people disturbed my life like a plow cutting through hard ground. Others came along and patiently picked stones that had cluttered the surface of my life. One or two spread smelly stuff they called fertilizer over me. That was hard to appreciate. And then came the seeds, made up of words and deeds that fell into the furrows

Backward glances can't change the past, but they can influence the present and future.

The mirror of memory helps prevent repeated mistakes.

of my heart and mind and germinated by a timetable all their own.

Rains came. Days and sometimes years passed. Here and there, in the field of me, seedlings of change broke the surface and grew into new habits, mature obedience, ripened wisdom. It took time, but I now see it as a picture of God's patience. He was working behind the scenes so undeniably that sometimes I think I see his shadow, hovering over my days, making all the difference. I am filled with gratitude for all those who planted into my life in God's name. How can I not do the same for the people God allows me to meet along the way? ✝

Here and there, in the field of me, seedlings of change broke the surface and grew into new habits, mature obedience, ripened wisdom.

*Every one of God's children
has a spiritual ancestry. How can
you thank those people who
planted God's Word in your life?*

*Who are you sowing the seeds of
the gospel in right now?*

THE TOUCH

Jesus turned around and said to her,
"Daughter, be encouraged! Your faith has made you well."
And the woman was healed at that moment.

— M ATTHEW 9:22

We are all healers who can reach out and offer health,

and we are all patients in constant need of help.

— HENRI NOUWEN,
DUTCH WRITER AND PASTOR

THE TOUCH

MATTHEW 9:22

They called themselves doctors, but they couldn't help me. Some of them sincerely tried, others pretended or even lied to me, but all of them expected payment. I spent everything I had for a service never rendered.

As men, they couldn't understand my shame or pain. Even the kind ones didn't recognize how their efforts frayed my dignity. By the time they were done looking, prodding, and asking, there was little left of me but tatters. The crimson rags that were my daily

lot seemed to take over my life.

No, it didn't hurt to bleed all the time, but feeling life seep away day after day caused an aching beyond words. What should have been an occasional reminder of my privilege to bear life became a continuous mockery that made living unbearable.

When I first heard the name Jesus and the word "physician" in the same sentence, my soul contracted in fear. Not another disappointment. The flicker of hope in me couldn't

bear such exposure. The slightest wind of failure would have extinguished it.

So I tried to sneak up on Jesus. If he was anything like his reputation, I thought, he could help me without even noticing. Couldn't I just be an anonymous patient? Terrified, I approached him in the pressing masses. The whole world seemed to want his attention. I just wanted to believe that he could free me from my humiliation. When Jesus passed me in the crowd, I reached out and touched his cloak. A shock of warmth and life flowed into me. I closed my eyes tightly and tears instantly formed on the tips of my lashes. Before I could even whisper in wonder, I heard him say, "Who touched me?"

The crimson rags that were my daily
lot seemed to take over my life.

Everything stopped. I almost burst out laughing. Of course he knew. The crowd wondered what he meant, and some even mocked his question. Meanwhile, he looked at me with eyes that spoke volumes about his understanding. I had just exchanged my unspeakable pain for his boundless life. Other healers had asked a thousand questions I couldn't answer; he asked one to which I had to reply. I stood before him and told my story, unashamed of my past in the glow of his acceptance. He used my tiny flame of faith to work a wonder in me.

The burden of pain that drove me, broken, to Jesus, I now see as a gift for which I am eternally grateful. His healing went immeasurably beyond what I ever dared to hope. ✝

Meanwhile, he looked at me with eyes that spoke volumes about his understanding.

I had just exchanged my unspeakable pain for his boundless life.

Jesus can heal your brokenness,
but first you must reach out to him.

In what ways are you still a patient?
In what ways can you become a healer?

THE STORM

He saw that they were in serious trouble,
rowing hard and struggling against the wind and waves.
About three o'clock in the morning he came to them,
walking on the water.

— MARK 6:48

Lord Jesus Christ, our God, the worries

and cares of our lives beat up against us in great waves.

Help us to see thee walking over the surging waters.

— PRINCESS ILEANA OF ROMANIA,
ARCHDUCHESS OF AUSTRIA

THE STORM

MARK 6:48

Jesus and his disciples? I knew them. I used to fish with some of the boys, before they followed Jesus. Later, they borrowed my boat many times. And they always brought it back. I was amazed at the storms they sailed through. Galilee sure has a mean streak! The howling winds and thundering surf they survived made those of us on shore glad we were smart enough to stay home. If my boat could talk, what stories she could tell. Instead, we often flipped her over on the beach and leaned against her as we sat by the fire. Simon, or should I say, Peter, kept us entertained during long nights by retelling some of his adventures with Jesus.

We never tired of laughing at Peter. His stories sounded like tall tales until he got to his part in them. The joke was always on him. Something in the way he described his bumbling and stumbling during incredible events always made them sound true. We listened, straight-faced and spellbound, as he told about Jesus' late-night stroll among the waves. We

74

burst into gales of laughter as Peter, with a wry grin, described his own brief experiment with walking on water.

The miracles Peter described were certainly memorable. With Jesus, they never seemed out of place, though. Jesus did unexpected and amazing feats, but his actions always fit with everything else we knew about him. He multiplied bread and fish one afternoon and walked on the water that night. The disciples were not only amazed by what Jesus did, but by the fact that his actions had never occurred to them in advance.

That was certainly true of the famous wave-walk. Jesus sent the disciples off in my boat without telling them how he would rejoin them. They didn't ask. If any of them wondered, they were soon distracted by a vicious storm. I don't know who was more afraid, the uneasy disciples who weren't fishermen or the

The disciples were not only amazed by what Jesus did, but by the
fact that his actions had never occurred to them in advance.

four fishermen who knew the terror of what could happen on Galilee. The fishermen rowed and shouted instructions; the rest bailed against the waves surging over the gunwales. Twelve men shared in that desperate fellowship.

Then one of the rowers caught sight of something moving behind them among the waves. He shouted in surprise and shock. Others joined him with their own cries of fear. What could this be? A shaft of moonlight illuminated the approaching figure. He looked like Jesus. Before they could speculate, he spoke, identifying himself.

The point, of course, wasn't that Jesus could walk on water (which Peter humorously illustrated), but that Jesus was the Son of God. Even those closest to him had to continually re-discover this truth. Those of us who stayed back on shore had to discover it, too. By the way, what have you discovered about Jesus? ✞

The point, of course, wasn't that Jesus could walk

on water . . . , but that Jesus was the Son of God.

Whatever difficulty you might be facing, Jesus is ready to come to your aid—perhaps in the most unexpected way.

Take a moment to recall God's past interventions on your behalf. Thank him for his faithful mercy and love.

MERCY

Then Jesus stood up again and said to her,
"Where are your accusers? Didn't even one of them condemn you?"
"No, Lord," she said. And Jesus said,
"Neither do I. Go and sin no more."

—JOHN 8:10-11

Christ is the ocean, in which every drop is infinite compassion.
He is the mountain towering above the mountains,
in which every grain is God's own goodness.
— HENRY LAW, ANGLICAN DEAN

MERCY

JOHN 8:10-11

Everything happened so quickly. I was with one of my regulars, a well-known married man, when several temple guards burst in the room. They had been waiting outside. Rudely pulling me out of bed and to my feet, they shoved me out the door. I glanced back and saw a smirk on the face of the man still sitting in bed, apparently content that he wouldn't be arrested too.

In the street, a small crowd of officials waited. My customer's urgent message had been a trap. The men cursed and threatened me, but their anger seemed fueled by someone else.

I tried to hold my clothing together as they shoved me in the direction of the temple. Women like me were often used and condemned by the same group. I stood there humiliated and very afraid. To those assembled, I was only an object, a thing. I knew they could kill me if it suited their purposes. I was trapped.

Those holding my arms steered me toward a large group gathered inside the temple courts. A man I had never seen before was

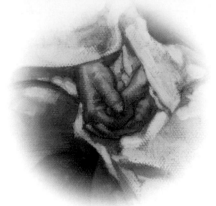

teaching. Nearby stood a group of religious leaders, awaiting our arrival.

Someone pushed me, and I fell between the teacher and the crowd. When I looked up, I noticed many men already had stones in their hands. Then one of the leaders announced to the teacher that I had been caught in the act of adultery. Should I be stoned, as Moses clearly commanded? I couldn't breathe.

Others repeated the question, demanding an answer from the man they called Jesus.

I turned to look at him and was shocked to find that he had crouched down beside me and was making marks in the dust. I couldn't read, so I didn't know what he was writing. But as the crowd continued to shout, he glanced briefly at me.

No one had ever looked at me that way. His eyes seemed to search my soul. I sensed his awareness of everything about me, and something else that frightened me even more than the stones hovering around us—to him I was

Someone pushed me, and I fell between the teacher and the crowd.
When I looked up, I noticed many men already had stones in their hands.

not an object. My life mattered, and suddenly I saw clearly how I had misused it.

As Jesus stood, the noise died down. Then he spoke: "All right, stone her. But let those who have never sinned throw the first stones!"

Even then I was immediately struck, not by the death sentence he had just delivered, but by the way he spoke the words. What seemed like judgment toward me was actually judgment on those who were demanding my death.

Crouching beside me again, he resumed writing. I heard the sounds of stones dropping and feet departing. I saw a faint smile on Jesus' face as he helped me stand. Suddenly, the judgment of others no longer mattered to me. I only wanted to know where I stood with Jesus. When he said, "I don't condemn you either; go and sin no more," I knew I had been given a second chance by the only one who could have justly stoned me. ✝

I sensed his awareness of everything about me, and something else that frightened me even more . . .
to him I was not an object. My life mattered, and suddenly I saw clearly how I had misused it.

We are all sinners, "caught in the act"
by God if by no one else.
Thank God for his forgiveness.

Has anyone wronged you lately?
How can you extend God's grace to them?

BARTIMAEUS

"I don't know whether he is a sinner," the man replied.
"But I know this: I was blind, and now I can see!"

—JOHN 9:25

Whoso loves believes the impossible.

—ELIZABETH BARRETT BROWNING,
ENGLISH POET

BARTIMAEUS

JOHN 9:25

My ears functioned very well. They often made up for what I lacked in sight. So I heard the questions the disciples asked Jesus, "Teacher, why was this man born blind? Was it a result of his own sins or those of his parents?" The experience of being ignored by people commenting on my blindness wasn't new, but the assumption that I couldn't see because I or someone else had sinned was deeply offensive. It also exposed my own question about my life's purpose.

Yet Jesus' response shocked me. He didn't provide any of the usual answers; instead, he offered a surprising and positive alternative. I had never before heard my blindness referred to as an opportunity for others to see God's power. I had never thought of my darkness as anything other than God's punishment. But Jesus wasn't finished shocking me.

The next sound I heard was someone spitting; then, after a moment, I sensed he was standing less than an arm's length from me.

Before I could say or do anything, a wet, sticky substance was smoothed over my eyes. I smelled mud. I heard snickers from onlookers. Then Jesus spoke again, "Go and wash in the pool of Siloam."

Siloam was nearby, and I knew the streets by heart. I had no reason to question Jesus' command, though I had no inkling of what would come from it. I made my way to the pool in such a hurry that I tripped over the lip and fell headlong into the waters. The mud on my face had dried a little, so I kept my face below the surface as I wiped away the crust from my eyes.

As I did so, I noticed an almost painful brightness where before I had known only darkness. I rose in surprise and found myself face to face with a friend whose voice I recognized immediately—Jesus. I was seeing him for the first time. So that's what faces, water, trees, buildings, and my own hands looked like! Someone was shouting praise to God, and I realized it was me, babbling about the

Yet Jesus' response shocked me. He didn't provide any of the usual answers;

instead, he offered a surprising and positive alternative.

wonder of everything. I closed my eyes for a moment, but I couldn't bear the darkness. I opened them again to the flood of light and felt hot tears flow. The power of God was something to see!

Before I could get out of the water I heard the questions begin: "Can he really see?" "Impossible. What kind of trick is this?"

That was only the beginning. I was prodded, doubted, threatened by people who should have been rejoicing with me. Instead, they seemed to wish that I had stayed in the dark, because that was more theologically acceptable than a blind person getting sight. I began to realize that a lot of people had a problem with what had happened. They didn't want to believe in Jesus, and my healing made that more difficult for them.

As for me, I was simply sure of one amazing truth—I got up blind in the morning, and by the evening I could see. I owed everything to Jesus! ☩

Someone was shouting praise to God, and I realized it was me,

babbling about the wonder of everything. . . . The power of God was something to see!

Reflect on this simple, eloquent
testimony: "I know this:
I was blind, and now I can see!"

Like the blind man, your personal
story of faith is powerful.
How has God healed you?

THE PRODIGAL

So he returned home to his father.
And while he was still a long distance away, his father saw
him coming. Filled with love and compassion, he ran
to his son, embraced him, and kissed him.

— LUKE 15:20

God's love is not drawn out by our lovableness, but wells up,

like an artesian spring, from the depths of his nature.

—JOHN HENRY JOWETT,
CONGREGATIONAL MINISTER

THE PRODIGAL

LUKE 15:20

I was angry. The more I thought about the situation, the more I was consumed with rage. A seething tide threatened to drown me. At first it was all about my little brother. How could he reject us like that? How could he waste so much? And how did he have the gall to come crawling back with nothing, begging for forgiveness? Then it was about my father. How could he let my brother go? Why did he give him so much? How could he take that messed-up kid back after all he had done?

Finally, it was about me. Did my father realize how frustrating it was to be the oldest? I felt trapped by feelings of responsibility. Sure, I stood to get the biggest share of the inheritance, but I also would get all the headaches of a large estate. Maybe, I thought, I could walk away from it all like my brother. Perhaps I could leave, too, and squander a fortune. But maybes were just my way of thinking without doing. I resented my life, and I resented the way I was.

So, I blew up at my father when my brother wandered home. His return brought me no joy, though I knew it should have. We were different, but still brothers—that should have been enough. But it wasn't. I brooded about the injustice and marveled at the party my father threw for him. I was in no mood to welcome him home. I withdrew from the party and hurt both my father and my brother by my ungratefulness, spite, and selfishness.

Later, I found myself alone, in a pigsty of my own making. I felt smeared with the filth of ingratitude. My cherished resentments had turned bitter in my mouth, impossible to swallow. I knew that I had to go back. I didn't deserve my father's love either, and I heard pride whisper that his love didn't await my return. Fear choked my heart. But then I

Finally, it was about me. Did my father realize how frustrating it was

to be the oldest? I felt trapped by feelings of responsibility.

remembered the longing on my father's face as he waited for my brother. I knew he would look at me with the same face.

So I, the older brother, wandered back too. I felt my shame deeply, for I should have known better. While still far from home, I saw an amazing sight. Dad was standing in the same place he had waited for my brother. He ran toward me with outstretched arms. He muffled my apologies and promises in the folds of his robe and wept with joy over me. I heard the sound of running footsteps and soon felt my little brother's hearty embrace. Now it was his turn to welcome me home. Through tearful sobs and hugs, I heard my father say, "I just knew we would be able to use that other fatted calf for a party some day." ✞

My cherished resentments had turned bitter in my mouth,

impossible to swallow. I knew that I had to go back.

No matter how far you wander
from your heavenly Father, he is always
eager to welcome you back.

Is there an area of your
life in which you need to confess
and return to God?

Poor Widow's Offering

*Then a poor widow came by and dropped in two pennies.
"I assure you," [Jesus] said, "this poor widow has given more than all
the rest of them. For they have given a tiny part of their surplus,
but she, poor as she is, has given everything she has."*

— L U K E   2 1 : 2 - 4

The world says, The more you take, the more you have.

Christ says, the more you give, the more you are.

— FREDERICK BUECHNER,
PRESBYTERIAN MINISTER
AND SPIRITUAL WRITER

POOR WIDOW'S OFFERING

LUKE 21:2-4

I didn't want the others to see me. I tried to be invisible as I passed through the crowd and found my place. I was ashamed of my status, embarrassed by my shabby clothes, and disappointed that I had so little to give when God had been so good to me.

Recent experiences had been discouraging. Those who did notice me didn't seem to understand, disbelieving my joy and insisting on offering their shallow sympathy. They seemed to doubt my smiles. I read the questions in their eyes. You're a widow—how are you going to make it? You can't think God's been fair, can you? You've got nothing, so what reasons do you have for being grateful to God? How can you be joyful when life has been so cruel? I was tired of their unspoken questions and judgment. I wanted to quietly slip my offering in the container and disappear.

While waiting in the offering line, I became aware of the noises. Voices filled the air with comments, arguments, questions, and

laughter. Somehow above all that volume I heard another sound—treasure. Silver rings when it bounces off the sides of the huge brass container in the temple. Gold proudly boasts its value with a clang against the offering bowl. I looked down at the two copper coins in my hand and knew they would announce their arrival with only a dull clink.

Then it was my turn. I dropped my coins and turned away quickly when I noticed someone watching me. Expecting derision, doubt, or pity, I looked into eyes that understood

I was ashamed of my status, embarrassed by my shabby clothes,

and disappointed that I had so little to give when God had been so good to me.

everything. Beneath those eyes I could see a smile that warmed my soul. Then he began to speak to those nearby, saying something about my offering. But the line behind me pushed me on, and I didn't catch everything he said. I didn't need to. He knew why I was there, and he was glad for me. I walked away thinking about how much I had just received. I knew my gift was accepted. I realized I was accepted too. I had to learn more about that man. ✝

I dropped my coins and turned away quickly when I noticed someone watching me.

Expecting derision, doubt, or pity, I looked into eyes that understood everything.

When have you, like the poor widow,
given sacrificially to God?

Does God have your best,
your all—or is there something
that you're withholding?

THE SERVANT

"And since I, the Lord and Teacher, have washed your feet,
you ought to wash each other's feet.
I have given you an example to follow.
Do as I have done to you."

— JOHN 13:14-15

Jesus Christ served others first; he spoke to those to whom no one spoke;

he dined with the lowest members of society; he touched the untouchable.

He had no throne, no crown, no bevy of servants or armored guards.

A borrowed manger and a borrowed tomb framed his early life.

— CHARLES W. COLSON,
FOUNDER OF PRISON FELLOWSHIP
MINISTRIES

THE SERVANT

JOHN 13:14-15

I watched Dad give so much to people, and I often wondered what kept him going. I knew he felt discouraged. I knew he failed at times. Life knocked him down and kicked him more than once, but he always got up. He was respected by some, reviled by others, but he made a difference in people's lives. His quiet persistence amazed me. So, during one of my own rough times in adolescence, I asked him about the secret to his endurance.

"I was hoping we would get around to talking about this some day," he said. Then he told me what it felt like to be alone in prayer, talking to Jesus. "There's something Jesus does for me, almost every time I get alone with him and pray about the challenges in my life," he said with a smile. "He doesn't just sit and listen to me. It's like, while he's listening, he sets a jug of hot water and a basin on the floor. As I pour out my heart to him, he pours the water in the basin and takes off my shoes. I'm humbled by his humility. I cry as I watch those wounded

hands, cleansing and soothing my feet."

"Does he say anything?" I asked, deeply touched by the picture.

"He listens. Sometimes he looks at me, and I remember things he's already said in his Word that apply to my complaint or struggle.

Much of the time, though, he's attentively silent. When he's done with my feet, he puts my socks and shoes back on, picks up the basin and towel, and stands. As he turns to go, he smiles at me and says, very quietly, 'Follow me.' That's really what keeps me going, son."

His quiet persistence amazed me. So, during one of my own

rough times in adolescence, I asked him about the secret to his endurance.

Dad taught me a lot about Jesus by the way he lived. Along the way, we had many conversations. I felt myself being molded. Even now, years after my final farewell to Dad, I still practice some of his habits. When I'm feeling overwhelmed, I go into my study alone and sit before my heavenly Father in prayer. I know I will find understanding and relief in that quiet place.

After a little while, the door opens and Jesus walks in, carrying his basin and towel. When I see him, I know I can keep going too. ✝

"As he turns to go, he smiles at me and says, very quietly,
'Follow me.' That's really what keeps me going, Son."

Jesus spun the galaxies, formed the earth, breathed life into humanity—and willingly stooped to wash his disciples' feet.

Are you a servant of the Servant?

JESUS' PRAYER

"My prayer is not for the world, but for those you have given me,
because they belong to you. ... I am praying not only
for these disciples but also for all who will ever
believe in me because of their testimony."

—J O H N 1 7 : 9 , 2 0

*He who has learned to pray has learned
the greatest secret of a holy and happy life.*

—WILLIAM LAW,
ANGLICAN SPIRITUAL WRITER

JESUS' PRAYER

JOHN 17:9, 20

I've been thinking, Lord, about my struggle to pray. So often, I can trace my reluctance to talk with you to some kind of disappointment. When life doesn't go quite the way I want, I frankly hold you responsible. I mean, if you can do anything, why don't you do what I ask?

Now I know that last question doesn't make sense. Even I realize how much trouble I would get into if you acted like a genie who answered my every wish. If I had that kind of clout with you, I would soon forget who is really in charge. I might even think I was somehow the center of the universe.

But admitting that you get the last word when it comes to answering prayer doesn't particularly help me with my disappointments. Maybe I need to take another look at my expectations. Perhaps I'm assuming you made promises or guarantees that you never made. Certain unanswered prayers or unexpected turns of events frustrate me when they shouldn't. They are actually exactly what you said would happen.

I'm reminded of your conversation with Peter during the Last Supper. I can almost hear you say, "Simon, Simon, Satan has asked to have all of you, to sift you like wheat. But I have pleaded in prayer for you, Simon, that your faith should not fail. So when you have repented and turned to me again, strengthen and build up your brothers." That couldn't have been good news for Peter. He didn't expect to fail, yet you told him to expect just that. You promised you had already prayed for him, not that he wouldn't fall flat on his face, but that his faith would not fail. I admit I'm like Peter. I'd like to skip all failures and suffering and go directly to spiritual success.

You did something similar a little later during the same meal. You made a statement I don't like to think about: "Here on earth you

If I had that kind of clout with you, I would soon forget who is really in charge.

I might even think I was somehow the center of the universe.

will have many trials and sorrows." This time you followed up the bad news with a guarantee that you had already overcome the world. That's when you prayed for the disciples and "for all who will ever believe in me because of their testimony." In other words, you prayed for me. You had me in mind on your last night here, just as you had me in mind on the Cross. In every life experience I can say,

"Jesus prayed for me in this situation, that my faith would not fail. How can I not keep going, even through disappointments and failures?" Every time I pray, I can be grateful that you have already anticipated my needs and struggles in prayer.

Forgive me, Lord. My real struggle with prayer involves my lack of deep gratitude. ✟

You had me in mind on your last night here,

just as you had me in mind on the Cross.

As a child of God, one for whom
Jesus continues to intercede, you
need never fear failure.

Does your life demonstrate
your gratitude to him?

JESUS IN THE GARDEN

Then an angel from heaven appeared and strengthened him.

— LUKE 22:43

Either he will shield you from suffering or he
will give you unfailing strength to bear it.
Be at peace, then, and put aside all anxious thoughts.
— FRANCIS DE SALES, FRENCH BISHOP

JESUS IN THE GARDEN

LUKE 22:43

The rest of us waited back among the trees. We were exhausted, but I also felt restless. Jesus had left us alone when he went off a little distance with Peter, James, and John. I could tell that he had even moved away from them to be by himself. Curious, I moved closer and listened as Jesus fell to his knees and cried out to God. Such passion in his voice! I was so used to hearing Jesus talk in tones of gratitude and confidence to his Father that it stunned me to hear his agony as my Lord poured out his heart.

The night sounds softened as if all creation were listening. I looked at the other disciples, my friends, settled on the ground, leaning against trunks, and wrapping their cloaks around them. Their mumbling and scuffling receded until I could distinctly hear Jesus' words as whispers in the shadows. The moonlight fell like a cascade that poured over his face. Tears streamed down his cheeks and glistened in the moonbeams. "Father, if you are willing, please take this cup of suffering away from me.

Yet I want your will, not mine," he pleaded. The night chill sent a shiver through me.

Jesus' words were troubling and comforting in ways I can't explain. I was exhausted because of the long day, the crowds, the meal, and the whirlwind of emotions we had experienced. Jesus had seemed determined to convince us he was about to die. Now he was telling God that even he didn't like the idea.

Why, I thought, would Jesus do anything he didn't want to do? Yet the tone of calm submission reverberating in the darkness that night stilled my own soul.

I lowered my head on my arms as I sat against a tree. Struggling against sleep, I closed my eyes. Moments later I opened them to what I thought must be a dream. Jesus was no longer alone. I squinted to see who was there.

Curious, I moved closer and listened as Jesus fell to his knees
and cried out to God. Such passion in his voice!

Standing behind him, a dim figure was assisting Jesus to raise his hands toward heaven. I shook my head. Could one of the others have slipped by me to offer the Lord companionship and comfort? A quick glance around confirmed what I already knew. The rest were slumbering behind me. When I turned back I could no longer see the figure and concluded it might have been some kind of vision. As I considered that, my eyelids slowly closed again, ignoring my commands to stay open.

"Get up and pray," were the next words I heard. Jesus was standing near me, speaking over my head toward my sleeping companions. In the distance I could hear the sounds of many feet and muffled voices. The chill returned.

Why, I thought, would Jesus do anything he didn't want to do? Yet the tone of calm submission reverberating in the darkness that night stilled my own soul.

God's will for your life may
not always be pleasant.
Will you follow him anyway?

What difficulty is God asking
you to pass through right now?

PETER DENIES JESUS

But Peter said, "Man, I don't know what you are talking about." And as soon as he said these words, the rooster crowed. At that moment the Lord turned and looked at Peter. Then Peter remembered that the Lord had said, "Before the rooster crows tomorrow morning, you will deny me three times." And Peter left the courtyard, crying bitterly.

— LUKE 22:60-62

*Courage is not simply one of the virtues but the
form of every virtue at the testing point.*

— C.S. LEWIS, SCHOLAR AND
PROLIFIC CHRISTIAN WRITER

PETER DENIES JESUS

LUKE 22:60-62

Last Sunday evening I was invited to a friend's house. As he often does when the nights turn cool, he pulled out a portable fire pit and had some logs blazing by the time we arrived. The crackling sounds and showers of sparks made a pleasing backdrop for conversation. With the exception of a couple of newcomers, the group consisted of old friends from work. I expected to relax.

"Catch, Pete," my friend said as he tossed my favorite ice-cold beverage. I popped the top, took a sip, and leaned back in the lawn chair. I couldn't think of a better way to unwind after a busy day.

I had been up early to pray with several other men from church. What had begun as a committed group, interceding for the ministry of the church, had deteriorated over the months into a yawning informal meeting during which the coffee got more attention than God. I was absent for several weeks and hadn't missed it. But after an attack of guilt, I showed

up that morning. The prayer time seemed a little more focused, but I still yawned through it.

Sunday service began after the prayer meeting. The pastor's sermon was entitled "Watch and Pray," but I thought about prayer so much that I really didn't pay attention to the "watch" part of the message. The adult Sunday school class had a half-hearted discussion about why Christians weren't making a bigger impact in society. It seemed to me that was society's problem, not ours.

All this reflecting made me yawn, and I took another sip of my drink. My friend commented, "Pete, that's the third or fourth yawn from you. We boring you? Don't you get enough sleep on Sundays? It's the one day I really get some rest."

I could have admitted that my problem wasn't getting up too early on Sundays but staying up too late on Friday and Saturday. Instead, I dodged the question. "Hey, I'm not bored. Just relaxed." Another friend joined the conversation, "That reminds me, Pete, you missed the pre-game show again today. What

What had begun as a committed group, interceding for the ministry of the church, had deteriorated over the months into a yawning informal meeting during which the coffee got more attention than God.

do you actually do on Sunday mornings?"

"Well," I answered without really thinking, "I like to take it easy on Sunday mornings. Besides, the pre-game shows always mess with my predictions and get me upset."

That's when one of the newcomers spoke up. "You know, I visited that church over on Maple Street this morning, and I could have sworn I saw you there."

It was an innocent comment. Yet I felt uncomfortable. For a moment it occurred to me that the people I worked with every day of the week didn't know what I did on Sundays or why I did it. They didn't know what I believed or whom I believed in. Then I said, "People often say that about me. There must be a lot of guys who look like me running around."

Just then my friend dropped another log on the fire and a shower of sparks leaped into the night sky. The conversation moved on to other things. Off in the distance, I heard the haunting, clear sounds of a solitary church bell, pealing out the hour. ✟

For a moment it occurred to me that the people I worked with every day of the week didn't know what I did on Sundays or why I did it. They didn't know what I believed or whom I believed in.

We've all denied Jesus at one time
or another, through what we've said
or done—or what we've left
unsaid or undone.

What keeps you from faithfully and
boldly standing up for Jesus?

CHRIST BEFORE PILATE

Pilate asked him, "Aren't you going to say something?
What about all these charges against you?"
But Jesus said nothing, much to Pilate's surprise.

— MARK 15:4-5

Before we can begin to see the cross as something done for us,

we have to see it as something done by us.

—JOHN STOTT,
PREACHER AND EVANGELIST

CHRIST BEFORE PILATE

MARK 15:4-5

My schedule was already packed, filled with questions to answer and problems to solve. Yesterday's leftover cases hung over my head and pressed down on me. In fact, my entire past seemed to hover like an invisible cloud. I had no time for interruptions. Then someone shoved Jesus through the doorway of my chambers.

He stood before me unwelcome, unwashed, wounded, bleeding, and very quiet. The look in his eyes was neither challenging, nor prideful, nor even fearful. Surely he understood I could dismiss him to death with a gesture. He faced me calmly, waiting. So many others had judged him. Now it was my turn.

The bindings on his wrists were probably as uncomfortable as the oozing cuts on his back and arms. On his forehead and cheeks, the blood from a deeply planted thorn-crown mixed with sweat to create pink streaks down his chin and neck. The swelling and bruising on his face distorted his appearance into an almost inhuman form. I found it difficult to

look at him. He met my gaze steadily, and I turned away.

Could I recuse myself? Others had tried only to discover that they had judged Jesus anyway. Should I dismiss the case? Plea-bargain to a lesser charge? Declare him innocent? Declare him guilty? I ruled out each option as unacceptable for different reasons. I was at an impasse.

Then I looked into his eyes again. He was appraising me. I suddenly realized that I had mistaken our roles in the encounter. I was not his judge; he was mine. I quickly reviewed the options I had just considered and wondered if he was using the same list. But I knew he wasn't indecisive. Where my judgments were frequently hedged and conditional, his judgment

He faced me calmly, waiting. So many others
had judged him. Now it was my turn.

would be truth. He saw the guilt and sin rooted in my very soul. My eyes closed in despair as I waited for him to ask for my plea. I couldn't bear his condemnation, because I had no excuse or alternative. The issue wasn't whether or not I was guilty, only what sentence he would pass.

Out of my pit of lostness I looked toward him again, and he spoke softly: "It was your weaknesses I carried; it was your sorrows that weighed me down. And you thought my troubles were a punishment from God for my own sins! But I was wounded and crushed for your sins. I was beaten that you might have peace. I was whipped, and you were healed!" His words described my imprisonment; then set me free. ✝

Then I looked into his eyes again. He was appraising me. I suddenly realized that
I had mistaken our roles in the encounter. I was not his judge; he was mine.

Jesus' identity remains on trial today.
He asks of every person,
"Who do you say that I am?"

We must each submit our judgment,
and what we decide will ultimately shape
our lives and determine our destinies.

So what is your ruling?
Who do you say that Jesus is?

The Cross

Then they nailed him to the cross.

— MARK 15:24

Christ took your cup of grief, your cup of the curse, pressed it to his lips,

drank in its dregs, then filled it with his sweet, pardoning,

sympathizing love, and gave it back for you to drink, and to drink for ever!

— OCTAVIUS WINSLOW,
MINISTER AND AUTHOR

THE CROSS

MARK 15:24

When I was younger I often wondered who was assigned the task of nailing Christ to the Cross. What was his name? How old was he? What did he look like? Was he reluctant to do it, or was it simply another command to be obeyed? Did he realize later, like the centurion, that Jesus was a righteous man? Did he repent?

I don't wonder any more. I know who nailed Jesus to the Cross. I know him intimately. It was I. In fact, I think it's impossible to become a Christian until the devastating realization hits you that you are responsible for putting Christ there on the Cross.

Something feels satisfying about driving home a large timber spike. The pin gives off a solid ring when it seats in the wood. The hammer handle rests comfortably in your hand, smoothed by countless grips. Many others have held this maul, but now it's your turn. The rough, forged nail in your other hand seems to weigh almost as much as the hammer. The spike becomes lighter when you rest its tip on the sur-

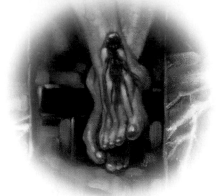

face you are about to pierce—a human hand.

You try to focus on the task before you. You know that some sick people actually enjoy this work, or they are so hardened that they do it without thinking, but you fit neither of those categories. You kneel with hammer and nail because of choices you made and choices God made.

Your choices created a debt you can't pay, a sin you can't atone, an offense you can't rem-edy. Judgment has been passed, and you have been declared guilty. The sentence is eternal separation from God. There is no higher court of appeal. You cast yourself at the mercy of the court.

God responds with terms that sound, at first, terrifying. The account must still be set-tled, the sentence carried out. Then he offers to take your place and suffer the ultimate pun-ishment on your behalf. "But," he adds, "you

I know who nailed Jesus to the Cross.

I know him intimately.

must nail me to the cross." You wonder how this can be, and God knows what you are thinking, so he says, "I will come to earth as a person just like you. I will show you how life should be lived, and I will live a sinless life When my work is done, you will nail me to a cross. I will take your place. Once you have let me do that, your sentence will have been met and you will be forgiven. There is nothing you can do to deserve this gift."

You will not nail Jesus to the Cross without getting his blood all over you. Sin-stains require unusual cleansing. The despicable nature of sin becomes clearer when we see its grisly consequences. By the time you have nailed Jesus' hands and feet, if you haven't been profoundly and eternally changed, you were only having a nightmare. ✝

"When my work is done, you will nail me to a cross. I will take your place.
Once you have let me do that, your sentence will have been met and you will be forgiven."

The Roman soldiers weren't working alone.
You helped them hold the hammer and
strike the nails, because it was your
sin, too, that Jesus died to pay for.

Ask Jesus to fill your heart with a
deep, abiding gratitude for his
sacrifice on your behalf.

RESURRECTION MORN

The guards shook with fear when they saw him,
and they fell into a dead faint.

— MATTHEW 28:4

Jesus lives! Thy terrors now

Can, O death, no more appall us;

Jesus lives! By this we know

Thou, O grave, canst not enthrall us.

Hallelujah!

— CHRISTIAN FURCHTEGOTT GELLERT,
GERMAN POET

RESURRECTION MORN

MATTHEW 28:4

I'm an old man now. You can't tell by looking at me, but I was once an intimidating Roman centurion, trained to stand my ground. And there wasn't much ground in the world I didn't consider mine. I believed I was part of an invincible army. We were the fierce and fearless muscle of the Empire.

During a tour of duty in Judea, however, I learned some painful lessons about my limitations. I discovered I was far from invincible. I found out my integrity had a price. I betrayed my salute as a Roman warrior to live by a code of duty and honor. In these last moments of my life, I want to set the record straight.

I remember feeling a little insulted when I got orders to guard the tomb of the crucified criminal named Jesus. What purpose could there be for guarding a grave? Certainly an executed convict didn't deserve the honor. What did they think? That he might try to escape? I would have protested the order, but my superior seemed shaken. He had super-

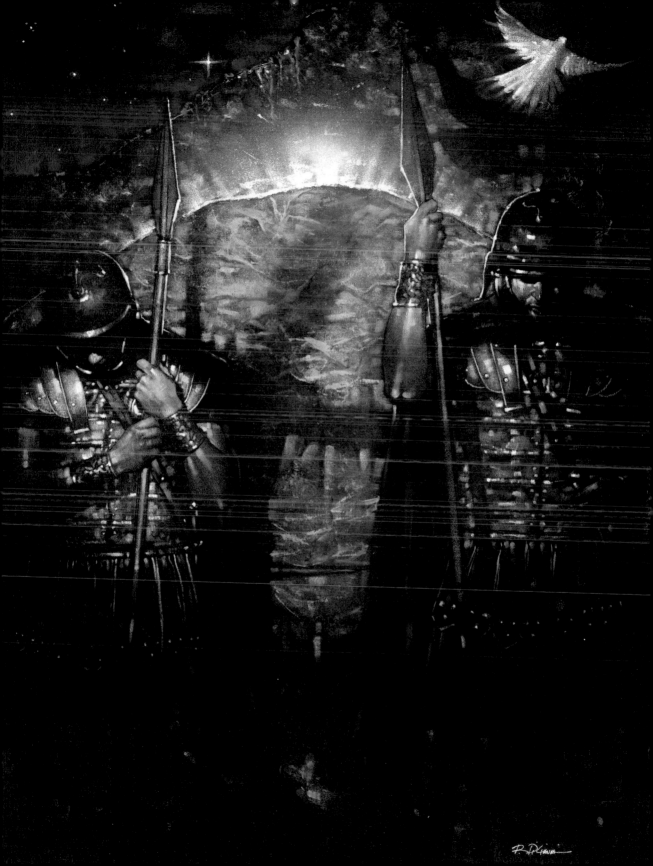

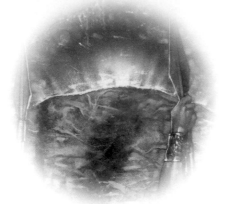

vised the crucifixions earlier that day. With blood still on his hands and uniform, he sat there muttering, "We killed a righteous man." I decided he was in no mood for arguments.

That night passed like a thousand other nights standing watch. We knew better than to hope that morning would come soon. We were tired but awake. Finally, as the early morning chill began to drive the sleep from our eyes, I heard an unusual sound like the flutter of wings. The earth started to shake. We automatically assumed our defensive positions, but the sound of attack came from behind us, the last place we expected. The massive stone sealing the grave began to roll aside. We spun to meet the enemy but were stunned at the sight. A huge, bright figure effortlessly moved the rock and leaned against it. His appearance alone defeated us. The rush of battle excitement evaporated. Our weapons fell from our shaking

I remember feeling a little insulted when I got orders to guard the tomb of the crucified criminal named Jesus.

hands, and we joined them, quaking in the dust.

Paralyzed by terror, I suddenly knew the tomb was empty. After a moment I heard women's excited voices and the heavenly being telling them to spread the news—Jesus was alive.

When the sounds receded, we rose sheepishly to our feet and made our way back into the city. Our report to the authorities elicited an unexpected response. They offered us money to spread the word that Jesus' followers had stolen the body. I admit I accepted the bribe. My pride as a soldier proved greater than my need as a sinner. I know I was wrong.

Jesus, I come to you no different than that man who hung next to you and asked you to remember him when you came into your kingdom. I'm just as lost and hopeless. Lord, remember me. I trust that the words of forgiveness you spoke from the Cross will also apply to me. ✤

I suddenly knew the tomb was empty. After a moment I heard women's excited voices

and the heavenly being telling them to spread the news—Jesus was alive!

According to Proverbs 9:10,
"Fear of the LORD *is*
the beginning of wisdom."

*Have you cultivated a healthy fear—
a reverent awe—for the resurrected
Ruler of the universe?*

FORGIVEN

*And since we have been made right in God's sight by the blood
of Christ, he will certainly save us from God's judgment. … We can
rejoice in our wonderful new relationship with God—all because
of what our Lord Jesus Christ has done for us.*

—ROMANS 5:9-11

*Jesus alone, by his divine power, was able to take on himself the
burden of the sins of the world. He carried it to the cross
where he offered himself as a sacrifice for our sins.*

—ORIGEN, EARLY CHRISTIAN
WRITER AND SCHOLAR

FORGIVEN

ROMANS 5:9-11

A lot happened the spring of my twelfth year. I was still young enough to enjoy the new dress I got for Easter, but old enough to resent my mother for not letting me choose it. Things were happening in me that I didn't understand, and the ups and downs in my relationship with Mom got higher and lower. We had more arguments. Sometimes I couldn't tell if I hated her or hated myself for having such feelings. The harder she tried, the easier it was for me to lash out at her. The storms between us showed no signs of clearing any time soon. Clouds of guilt hovered over me.

That Easter morning repeated our weekly church routine with the added yawn of a sunrise service. The new dress looked so nice that I wished I were wearing it to a more important place. By the time I arrived at Sunday school, the dress had lost some of its starched crispness, but at least it held its own with the outfits my friends were modeling. With giggles and unspoken comparisons, we gradually

settled down for the lesson. I noticed we had a new teacher that day.

In a soft voice, Katherine introduced herself. Accustomed to teachers who tried to out-shout our boisterous noisiness, we were surprised into listening by her quiet approach. Katherine laid several objects on the table. The first one was a wreath made from vines with sharp thorns. It took a moment for my years of church lessons to kick in and help me solve the puzzle. She had brought a crown of thorns. That made the large wooden mallet and railroad spikes easy to identify.

The teacher confirmed my guesses as she talked about each item. I was so pleased to be right that I only half-listened to her explanations. But then she said something that caught my attention. "We're here to remember the Resurrection, but I wonder, why did Jesus have to die in the first place?" Silence. I glanced at the clock. Class was almost over, but the question caused an unexpected discomfort in me.

Katherine let the silence hang for a moment. She didn't answer her question, as

"We're here to remember the Resurrection, but I wonder,

why did Jesus have to die in the first place?"

our teachers usually did. Instead, she said, "The answer to this question is very personal. I don't know if any of you are ready to think about it. I'm going to end class now, but if any of you want to stay and talk, I'd be happy to tell you more."

I kept my head bowed after her prayer, while the rest of the class scraped their chairs back and shuffled out. After it was quiet, I opened my eyes to find that only Katherine and I remained. She smiled and beckoned me to come to the table. I looked down as I approached and saw that there were two pieces of paper lying there. One had "Guilty" scrawled on it. The other had "Forgiven" written boldly above a signature I recognized even upside down—Jesus.

It was the strangest experience. Even before Katherine spoke, I felt as if someone had stepped behind me and was gently resting his scarred hands on my shoulders. I realized I was about to hear something that would change my life forever. ✚

I felt as if someone had stepped behind me and was gently resting his scarred hands on my shoulders.

Are you carrying a load of guilt?
Worried that your sins are
too deep for forgiveness?

Jesus places his scarred hands on
your shoulders and whispers,
"You are forgiven."

HE HOLDS
THE KEYS

I am the living one who died. Look, I am alive forever and ever!
And I hold the keys of death and the grave.

— REVELATION 1:18

Christ is the Morning Star who, when the night of this world is past brings to
his saints the promise of the light of life and opens everlasting day.
—VENERABLE BEDE, ENGLISH MONK

HE HOLDS THE KEYS

REVELATION 1:18

Word came to us in Ephesus that a ship bound for Crete would be making a supply stop at Patmos. I was asked to book passage for the island in hopes of finding out how our brother John was doing. His exile had been painful to all of us, and we longed to hear word of his health.

I arrived to find him on what I thought was his deathbed. The months of labor in the mines had taken their toll, but the weight of personal losses seemed a heavier burden than work. He was the last of the twelve and had witnessed or received news that each of his fellow apostles had been killed by blade, stone, or cross. Now he was weak, though an unquenchable fire seemed to shine in his eyes when he greeted me.

After a brief conversation, I hurried to the authorities and begged for John's release. I promised to arrange his transport back to Ephesus. I pointed out that in his state of health he was of no use to them in the mines anyway; he was only a burden on their meager stores of

food. The warden said he had often wondered why John was sent there in the first place. He never caused trouble and had been a calming effect on the other prisoners. "Why," he asked, "would someone who speaks continuously about love be seen as a threat to anyone?"

I ventured a response. "Sir, the one we follow was killed for speaking of love. Yet his love compels John to imitate him."

"Well, since I have a measure of discretion in these matters," the warden responded, "I will release John to your care."

When I returned to John with the good news, he chuckled. "He may think he has the keys to keep or release me, but I know better." He picked up a scroll by his bed. As he unrolled it, the new vellum exuded a rich, leathery odor. The creamy surface made the words that John had painstakingly written seem to jump off the page. Without touching the surface, he tracked the phrases until he came to a special one. Then he looked up at me, with a smile. "I have seen the Lord," he said in hushed tones. I read the words under his finger: "Don't be afraid! I am

He was the last of the twelve and had witnessed or received news that each of his fellow apostles had been killed by blade, stone, or cross.

the First and the Last. I am the living one who died. Look, I am alive forever and ever! And I hold the keys of death and the grave." Like a calming voice, those words from the Lord filled and stilled my soul.

"The one who holds the keys to death and the grave also holds the keys to life," John said, his resolve shedding the exhaustion and sickness from his glowing face. "This island prison is no match for his power. I didn't know you were coming, but I knew someone would arrive to take this revelation back to the churches. I didn't suspect I would get to travel with it back to the mainland, but I'm ready. The Lord has a final word for his church."

Keys have always fascinated me. They work in two directions—locking what is open and opening what is locked. Presumably, the one who has the keys knows what to do with them. Whatever side of the door I happen to be on isn't quite as important as knowing the one who holds the keys. My hope, in this life and the next, rests on him. ✝

Then he looked up at me, with a smile.
"I have seen the Lord," he said in hushed tones.

As Jesus' follower, the wonders and glories of heaven have been opened to you.

Reflect on the hope of heaven that Jesus has given to you.

The Messenger

Then I saw four angels standing at the four corners of the earth, holding back the four winds from blowing upon the earth. Not a leaf rustled in the trees, and the sea became as smooth as glass.

—REVELATION 7:1

Think of it! Multitudes of angels, indescribably mighty,
performing the commands of heaven! … Believers, look up—take courage.
The angels are nearer than you think.
—BILLY GRAHAM, EVANGELIST

THE MESSENGER

REVELATION 7:1

She recognized the figure in the painting, although I couldn't remember ever describing an angel to her. This recognition, of course, provoked a cascade of questions. I couldn't tell whether they came from sheer curiosity or her nightly mission to gain some extra minutes of awake time. But she asked with such eagerness that I found it impossible to disappoint her. I didn't have answers for all her questions, but I felt a fatherly duty to engage her inquisitiveness. I also knew my time was running out for passing on to her what others would later contradict.

"No, sweetheart," I began, "I've never seen an angel—at least not one who wasn't traveling under cover. I expect that heaven will give me a chance to find out just how many of God's messengers I've rubbed shoulders with or even ignored during my lifetime. That's one of the reasons your mom and I try hard to practice hospitality to strangers. God's Word tells us that some who entertain strangers end up

hosting angels without realizing it. Even if we never do serve an angel, we know it is still worthwhile to practice hospitality. Heaven will be a wonderful place partly because of all those friends who might otherwise have remained strangers. Hospitality is a head-start to heaven. . . .

"Yes, I do think we would recognize an angel if he showed himself to us as he appears in God's presence. This picture gives us some idea. The wings would catch our attention. But I think the artist toned down the angel's brightness for us, otherwise we couldn't see the angel's features. . . .

"Yes, I know people who have seen angels. They've written about what they saw and felt—mostly what they felt. They were afraid. Not because they thought the angel was going to hurt them, but because they realized the angel came directly from God. . . .

"God has used angels throughout history to

They were afraid. Not because they thought the angel was going to hurt them,
but because they realized the angel came directly from God.

tell people special, personal messages. Angels also will have a big part in the way that history comes to an end. The Bible has a number of stories about how angels helped, warned, and instructed people. Jesus even mentioned that special angels are assigned to watch over children. Now, doesn't that make you feel safe?"

As I was speaking I noticed our reflection in the window, a father probably telling his daughter more than she really wanted to know.

I paused, expecting another question, and then noticed that her breathing had changed. Long lashes lay softly on her cheeks as she dreamed a child's adventures. Somewhere along the line, my answers had changed from information to comfort, and she had drifted off.

As I tiptoed to the door and turned out the light, I thanked the Lord for his special messengers. I knew I wasn't the only one watching over my daughter that night. ✝

Somewhere along the line, my answers had changed from information to comfort, and she had drifted off.

Angels are all around us,
whether we realize it or not.

Take courage.
Angels are watching over you.

HEAVEN'S DOOR

There are many rooms in my Father's home,
and I am going to prepare a place for you.
If this were not so, I would tell you plainly.

—J O H N   1 4 : 2

Hearts on earth say in the course of a joyful experience, "I don't want this ever to end." But it invariably does. The hearts of those in heaven say, "I want this to go on forever." And it will. There is no better news than this.

— J. I. PACKER, THEOLOGIAN

HEAVEN'S DOOR

JOHN 14:2

o my children:

I love you. You are reading this letter because I have died. I hope these words will simply remind you of the way I tried to live. I know we won't speak again until you join me, but consider this a last wave goodbye from your dad beyond the final doorway.

I believe the contents of this letter are much more valuable and important than anything I stated in my will. That document recorded my wishes regarding the things of earth. This document records my wishes regarding the things of heaven. My will is about everything I left behind. This note is about what I took with me.

The one possession that went through death with me is my relationship with Jesus Christ. Everything else, including my own body, had to be left behind. Actually, I'm looking forward to a new model, because the old arms, legs, heart, and other miscellaneous parts were pretty much worn out anyway. I

believe I'll always be your mother's husband and your father, but even those relationships, as dear as they are to me, will be changed by eternity. What I have with Jesus, however, and the fact that he has me, will never change.

My relationship with Jesus, my Savior, filled me with three things that I trust you will remember and think about as you remember me. Jesus gave me faith, hope, and love. You and I know that I wasn't perfect in any of these. In fact, I know I was less perfect than you would ever guess. But Jesus gave me a dose of faith, hope, and love that made an everlasting difference in my life, even while I was still earthbound.

Remember how I often said that faith, hope, and love didn't exist in a vacuum? They require a relationship. The more I exercised faith, hope, and love in my relationship with Jesus, the more he poured out those qualities

My will is about everything I left behind.

This note is about what I took with me.

into my life. The way I treated each of you was meant to be an expression of the way Jesus treated me. I hope I never let you down.

I know that my death provoked sadness. That's one way we know we have loved—when we grieve the loss of the one we loved. But in grief, I don't want your hearts to be troubled. As Jesus said, "You trust God, now trust in me." I hope my life offered you a pretty good reason to trust in Jesus. But in light of my failures, please remember that Jesus is worthy to be trusted for his own sake.

This letter comes to you as my last living wish. I long to spend eternity with you. I hope I haven't given you any reason not to want that as well. But I also know this wish will only be fulfilled if you make your relationship with Jesus the one thing you take out of life with you. Until then …

Love,

Dad ✝

The more I exercised faith, hope, and love in my relationship with Jesus,

the more he poured out those qualities into my life.

As a follower of Jesus, an endless life of glory and joy is promised to you.

Does your life reflect your future hope?

SAFELY HOME

*Yes, we are fully confident, and we would rather be away from
these bodies, for then we will be at home with the Lord. ... [He will say],
"Well done, my good and faithful servant ... Let's celebrate together!"*

—2 Corinthians 5:8; Matthew 25:23

Finish then Thy new creation, Pure and spotless may we be;

Let us see Thy great salvation, Perfectly restored in Thee;

Changed from glory into glory, Till in heaven we take our place,

Till we cast our crowns before Thee, Lost in wonder, love, and praise.

— CHARLES WESLEY,
METHODIST HYMN WRITER AND PREACHER

SAFELY HOME

2 CORINTHIANS 5:8; MATTHEW 25:23

I have witnessed the scene countless times, yet I never tire of the wonder. The Lord certainly never tired of the moment. He anticipated each one as if it was the first and only. I was thrilled simply to be a minor participant in the grand occasions, waiting each time to step forward with my light burden.

Carefully draped over my arms lay the painfully white garments that would clothe the new arrivals. On top of each robe the Lord would place a magnificent crown whose jewels sparkled in the light. They projected on the walls the images of special acts of service, often unnoticed by the world, that were closely observed and eternally recorded here. The crown held the inscribed name of its owner and was fitted precisely to him or her, yet it was never worn. I've seen both the workshop and the magnificent storehouse where crowns of every size and shape were carefully displayed with honor. Each had incalculable value.

I stood ready, knowing that every person

who came would be amazed at their individual treatment. Each was scheduled for a personal welcome. Each would receive the undivided attention of the Lord. There was no hurry, no waiting, not a shred of anxiety. Time mattered not. In fact, time, as they knew it, no longer existed.

The sequence was always the same, yet infinitely varied. The new arrivals found the Lord seated on his throne, waiting. Surprised, shocked, and overwhelmed, they stood speech-less. Just a moment ago they had been bound by time and space; then, suddenly, they were thrust into eternity. Having left the confusing mix of pleasure, pain, and finitude, an existence they called life, they were now enveloped by the infinite; filled with the best of everything.

A great shout of welcome cascaded from the throne! Each one heard his or her name, spoken in tones of intimate, joyful familiarity. Drawn to the face they suddenly recognized, they flew across the carpet with arms out-

I stood ready, knowing that every person who came
would be amazed at their individual treatment.

stretched. Limbs and other body parts that may have been idle or missing for years instantly sprang into action as they rushed forward. But the One on the throne met them at the foot of the stairs. Oblivious of the beauties that surrounded them, each one fell at his feet speaking of praise, gratitude, humility, surprise, and more gratitude. He knelt and embraced them.

This was my signal, so I stepped forward as the Lord retrieved a crown. When these mar-tyred ones first saw their crowns, they smiled in recognition, for each jewel held a special memory. The Lord himself whispered honoring words to each person as he offered to crown them. But they always offered their crowns back to him in worship.

As the two embraced again, the Lord whispered, "Thank you, Father, for this one who is safely home." ✠

A great shout of welcome cascaded from the throne! Each one heard his or her name . . . Drawn to the face they suddenly recognized, they flew across the carpet with arms outstretched.

Someday your earthly body will be transformed into a glorious heavenly body. Your burdens will become joys, and Jesus himself will wipe away your tears.

What are you looking forward to most in the life ahead?

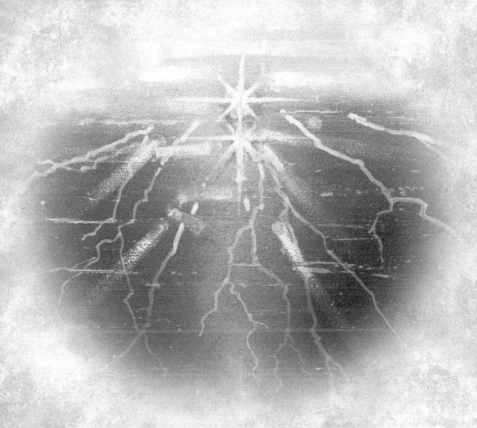

REVELATION 4

*And then at last, the sign of the coming of the Son of Man
will appear in the heavens, and there will be deep mourning among
all the nations of the earth. And they will see the Son of Man
arrive on the clouds of heaven with power and great glory.*

— MATTHEW 24:30

There will be little else we shall want of heaven besides Jesus Christ.
He will be our bread, our food, our beauty, and our glorious dress.
The atmosphere of heaven will be Christ; everything in heaven
will be Christ-like: yes, Christ is the heaven of His people.

— C.H. SPURGEON, BAPTIST MINISTER

REVELATION 4

MATTHEW 24:30

The spring morning dawned with a cloudless blue sky that promised warmer days ahead. But winter wasn't yet finished cleansing the world with cold. A slight but chilling breeze caused my eyes to water as I walked to the mailbox, disappointed to find it empty yet delighted by the opportunity to enjoy the crisp air. The aroma of fresh brewed coffee welcomed me back to the house, and I settled with a hot mug in front of the picture window overlooking the valley. Any day, a blush of green would sweep through our woods, and life would burst into sight everywhere. The view would be transformed into another vivid example of God's faithfulness. I couldn't help but wonder if Christ might return on a day like this one, a day when we were waiting for the promise that each spring brings.

I opened my Bible to Revelation 4, wanting to fill my imagination with the description of Christ's appearance. John's words exploded off the page like colorful fireworks. He used the palate of gemstone hues to paint his portrait,

and I could imagine how close he came to capturing what, in reality, must be indescribable. Jasper, carnelian, and emerald are not only precious for their rarity, but also for their color. The crystalline form of these jewels bends and splits the light passing through them, giving it vibrancy and life. What an apt description of the one who is both light and life, transforming all those in whom he dwells! No wonder John saw Christ as one who is never still, even when sitting on his throne in heaven. Flames, lightning, and thunder flowed from him while he received worship from those he created.

John framed Jesus in a rainbow, the sign of God's promise. The misty arches remind us of God's guarantee of safety, and they hearken back to his first promise of a Savior. As long as we remain in this world of shifting feelings, pain,

I couldn't help but wonder if Christ might return on a day like this one,

a day when we were waiting for the promise that each spring brings.

and disappointment, we will never feel entirely safe, for we have an unavoidable appointment with death. Yet God's promise of safety includes a dimension beyond this life, in which God will transform every evil into good. His promise in the garden of a remedy for sin anticipates his promise of safety in all of life's storms. Eventually, as John wrote, the sign of the promise will become the sign of the promise fulfilled.

I looked up from the pages with tear-filled eyes, overwhelmed by the comfort of Jesus' majesty. Sunlight poured in through the window as I gazed past barren branches to the brightness on the horizon. I half-expected to see what John saw so long ago. My hope was rekindled. *After all,* I thought, *it's only morning. He could still return today.*

God's promise of safety includes a dimension beyond this life,

in which God will transform every evil into good.

Angels never cease praising the
"one who lives forever and ever,"
the only Creator and King.

Take a moment to come before God's throne.
Join in the heavenly worship.

RON DiCIANNI

Ron DiCianni's Bible-based paintings are not so much illustrations of Scripture as they are powerful, visual meditations on God's Word. One distinctive aspect of his paintings is how they intimately draw viewers into the biblical stories, which is character-istically true in *Were You There?*.

For more than a quarter century, Ron DiCianni has been contributing a unique artistic vision to the world of art. By the end of the 1980s, he had established himself widely as an illustrator and commissioned artist with an international reputation. Although Ron has always considered his abilities a gift from God and has desired to honor God with the quality of his work, the last decade has marked an intentional shift in Ron's focus. He has dedi-cated himself to what he describes as "the Lord's call to help reclaim the use of visual arts within the church as part of worship and outside the church as part of evangelism."

Ron has published numerous books featuring his art and writing. These include *Beyond Words* (Tyndale, 1998), *A Brush with God's Word* (Tyndale, 2002), and *The Invitation* (Broadman & Holman, 2002). His artwork appears on the covers of *This Present Darkness, Piercing the Darkness,* and *Angel-walk* (Crossway). He has also partnered with such authors as Max Lucado, Joni Eareckson Tada, and Michael Card in producing the beloved *Tell Me* series of children's books (Crossway).

Ron is a native of Chicago and lives in California with his wife, Pat, and their two greatest works of art, their sons Grant and Warren.

NEIL WILSON

Raised in a family of missionary Bible translators, Neil Wilson's education included an interest in literature (Aurora University, B.A. English) and a commitment to biblical scholarship (Trinity Evangelical Divinity School, M.A. Religion). Until 2000 Neil's primary focus was youth and pastoral ministry, but he also contributed as a freelance writer to numerous publishing projects, including the best-selling *Life Application Study Bible* and *The Handbook of Bible Application* (Tyndale).

For the last four years he has worked for The Livingstone Corporation, a service provider for Christian publishers. He has collaborated with numerous authors in developing books, including Chip Ingram, Sue Mallory, Randy Pope, Ramesh Richard, and Dave Veerman. Most recently, Neil contributed to the devotional *His Passion* (Integrity, 2004).

Neil lives with his wife, Sherrie, near Oshkosh, Wisconsin, close to their three married children and three amazing grandchildren.